Ice Hours

Ice Hours

POEMS BY **MARION STARLING BOYER**

WHEELBARROW BOOKS ▪ *East Lansing, Michigan*

⊗ The paper used in this publication meets the minimum requirements
of ANSI/NISO Z39.48-1992 (R 1997) (Permanence of Paper).

Wheelbarrow Books
Michigan State University Press
East Lansing, Michigan 48823-5245

Library of Congress Control Number: 2022936916
ISBN 978-1-61186-449-6 (paper)
ISBN 978-1-60917-725-6 (PDF)
ISBN 978-1-62895-493-7 (ePub)
ISBN 978-1-62896-487-5 (Kindle)

Cover design by Erin Kirk
Cover art: Summer sunset in Antarctica, by Goinyk; Adobe Stock.

Visit Michigan State University Press at *www.msupress.org*

With the publication of Marion Starling Boyer's collection of poems, *Ice Hours*, the Residential College in the Arts and Humanities (RCAH) Center for Poetry at Michigan State University offers its eleventh book in our Wheelbarrow Books Poetry Series. Clearly, we pay homage to William Carlos Williams and his iconic poem, "The Red Wheelbarrow." Readers will remember the poem begins "so much depends upon . . ." that red wheelbarrow. As our number of Wheelbarrow Books increases, we hope that our audience increases also. Help us spread the word. In the beginning was the word, we're told, and the word became the poem. So much depends upon the collaboration of reader, writer, and poem, the intimate ways we come to know one another.

Just before the opening poem of Marion Boyer's incredible collection, *Ice Hours*, a story of the Imperial Trans-Antarctic Expedition offered from multiple perspectives, we are told that on August 14, 1914, Great Britain declares war on Germany and Ernest Shackleton is given permission to proceed with his expedition to sledge across the continent of Antarctica. In that opening poem, Antarctica speaks directly to the reader, sharing a bit of her history from the time she was tropical until she was covered with snow and ice. The poem ends

> I was tropical once.
>> Then, I became so cold
>
> I stripped off my clothes
>> and burrowed beneath a shield of ice.

Ice Hours is the story of men who signed on for this hazardous journey, their voices dredged up from the snow, the ice, the past by Marion Boyer, men who left behind their warm homes and comfortable lives only months later to find themselves burrowing beneath snow and ice in their attempt to stay alive surrounded by whiteness, then darkness, gale-force winds, ship-shattering ice packs, deaths of their necessary and beloved sled dogs, frostbite, and worse. Not all of them survive. We come to know them so well, so personally, so lovingly through Boyer's expertly crafted language and deep empathy that every loss, though sometimes expected, is a punch in the gut, a gasping for breath. For those who survive, we can't help but wonder what will come next, how they will recover from the psychological trauma and physical injury, though the *Times of London*, December 29, 1913, promised "honour and recognition in case of success."

Ice Hours could not be landing in our bookstores at a more crucial time as one of the two ships from Shackleton's expedition, the *Endurance*, stuck in the ice floes for ten months before the shifting ice crushed it and the crew attempted their trek across the ice, was discovered on March 5, 2022, exactly one hundred years after Shackleton was laid to rest. Much has already been made of the fine condition of the ship, submerged in frigid waters for a century where it could not be destroyed by various elements. It is hard for us to imagine what that 1914–1917 trek across the continent was like as we watch glaciers come crashing into the waters because of global warming and tourist expeditions travel into the once unsurvivable continent. Todd Plummer in the *Daily Beast* writes, "More than 74,000 tourists ventured to Antarctica during the 2019–20 season— up from 27,000 a decade ago—comfortably navigating waters that in the 1910s 'spelled almost certain doom.'" Families, children, retirees clamber into boats with hulls designed for icebreaking and polar cruises, sleeping in luxurious cabins, dining in elegant restaurants. This is not the world we encounter in *Ice Hours,* when men were paid small wages, spent months in total darkness, survived mostly on seal meat, and used the blubber for light and heat, trying desperately to get to the next hut or supply station before their resources, material and physical, were depleted. I remember watching a television show as a child hosted by Walter Cronkite, *You Are There.* His famous concluding line from each show went something like, "What sort of a day was it? A day like all days, filled with those events that illuminate and alter our time, but you were there."

We are there as Marion Boyer's skillful storytelling places us on a ship torn loose in a storm from its anchors; watch men, desperate for a smoke, fill their pipes with a mixture of tea leaves, coffee grounds, sawdust, and sennegrass, adding a few dried herbs ("It survived all criticism"); feel trapped in a twelve day blizzard, hear Richards say, "It would be very easy to die." Before the ships depart, we are at St. Pancras station hearing

The clatter of the morning crowds, rumbling
carts, vendors hawking war headlines; the screech
and hiss of locomotives, their monstrous chuffs,
billows of steam; whistles, wailing babies,
reverberating announcements. All the hubbub . . .

Pages and months later, it is

For the fifth day, the blizzard claws their two tents
smaller, crushes their bodies tighter together.
Shrieks rise and rise, rattle ribs, quake the bowels,

then die back. . . .

The four dogs curl in a torpor beneath deep snow.
There's no food left for them. Joyce exhausts himself
digging out channels for the dogs to keep breathing.

I read this manuscript four times, and each time I was as cold, as anxious, as bereft, and as amazed by Boyer's ability to transport me to a time a century ago where I feared for the survival of us all. Making the story more poignant, Boyer has interspersed the monologues of the explorers with the voice of Antarctica, letters to and from loved ones, updates from the war at home, and appropriate epigraphs from writers as varied as William Carlos Williams, Robert Service, Kelly Tyler-Lewis, and T. S. Eliot. In the final poem, when the men who have been wild and filthy for more than two years understand that the *Aurora* has appeared and they are rescued, the poet tells us, "In such a moment perhaps nothing seems / quite real, but the mind may just crack / open enough to allow a narrow glimpse / of something warm. Something clean." I am grateful to have made this trek, with these men, at a time long gone, a time never-to-be again. I am stronger for having witnessed their struggle against overwhelming odds. I am blessed to have been in the company of Marion Boyer's voice.

—ANITA SKEEN, *Wheelbarrow Books Series Editor*

Marion Starling Boyer's *Ice Hours* is mesmerizing and haunting. At its core is the question, what motivates people to want to be a part of something whose success seems impossible? This is acknowledged even in the recruitment of crew, offering "small wages, bitter cold, long months of complete darkness, constant danger, safe return doubtful." The book follows the Trans-Antarctic Expedition of 1914, whose goal was to make the first land crossing of the Antarctic continent. Poems explore the flora and fauna; crew and families; and the challenges, failures, and triumphs. It traces this journey from Antarctica where "pink-golden mists of pollen wafted across / deep valleys" to a winter freeze that sends "violent wind, black waves roiling." Boyer's precise language dazzles in portraits of historical figures; letters to a fiancée back in England; and descriptions of brutal weather, the sea, boats, animals, and people. There may be no answer to the central question of *Ice Hours*, but the reader is riveted by the vision and obsession that sparked this historic expedition.

—CAROL DAVIS

CONTENTS

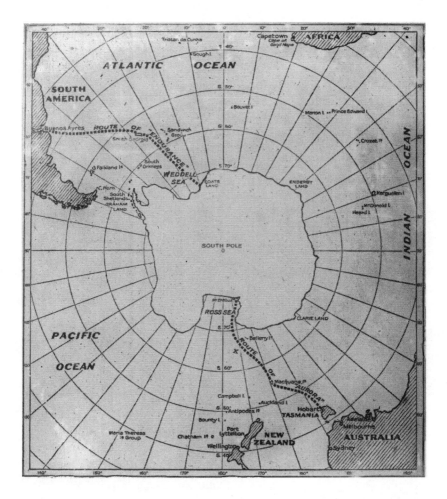

ROUTES OF *ENDURANCE* AND *AURORA*

Map shows route from South America to Antarctica of the
Endurance and the route from Tasmania to Antarctica of the *Aurora.*
Photo by Keith Jack (1885–1966), State Library Victoria.

Perhaps I Was Eden

Antarctica

I was tropical once. Warm,
    with the warming effect of clouds.

    My lands were fern-forests.
Araucaria trees rose high,
    baobabs grew fleshy-fat with water

    and rains came and drifted and came.
Warmth transported me.
    Slow rivers spooled soft.

Pink-golden mists of pollen wafted across
    deep valleys.
Rain. Muttered refrains.

    The green veils shifting
across the glinting nights
    are my dreams of that emerald time.

    My days are a season long;
night lasts half the way around our star.

There is no mythology here, only epochs.

It was ever slow, then slower.
    Leafy. Perhaps I was Eden.

I remember a sweet summons—
    something silken, secret;

    the sigh and sob of sea swells,
small spasms. An ache.

Snow.
A massive weight covered me, groaning.

A rhythm of crescendo. Arching.
I remember mountains rose. A tectonic lifting.
    Molten lava.

The last to survive were beech bushes.
    Then, the cool feathers of drowsing.
A slowed pulse. Fog.

    There is no mythology here.
My mountain still breathes. Plumes rise.

I was tropical once.
    Then, I became so cold

I stripped off my clothes
    and burrowed beneath a shield of ice.

ONE AUDACIOUS IDEA

The Imperial Trans-Antarctic Expedition

AUGUST 4, 1914. Great Britain declares war on Germany. Ernest Shackleton receives permission to proceed with his expedition to sledge across the continent of Antarctica.

DECEMBER 24, 1914. The *Aurora* departs Hobart, Tasmania, for Antarctica, a 2,500-mile voyage through the wild Southern Ocean that will take more than two weeks.

The simple things, the true things, the silent men who do things—
Then listen to the wild—it's calling you.

        —ROBERT SERVICE, "The Call of the Wild"

The programme involved some heavy sledging, but I had not anticipated the work would be extremely difficult.

        —ERNEST SHACKLETON, speaking of the Ross Sea party

One Audacious Idea

Men wanted for hazardous journey. Small wages, bitter cold,
long months of complete darkness, constant danger, safe
return doubtful. Honour and recognition in case of success.
—*TIMES OF LONDON*, December 29, 1913

London, September 1914

Spencer-Smith's cigarette smoke drifts up
to the iron ribs arched above St. Pancras
railway station. He inhales his Woodbine

and leans into the tight cluster of people
surrounding Ernest Shackleton who is reassuring
Victor Hayward's mother that he won't have
too much work on the expedition.

Hayward banters, *Surely this won't fizzle out
to be a picnic,* then grins at Ethel, his fiancée.

Victor's application, among the many thousands,
had been dropped into the best of three filing drawers
labeled *Mad, Hopeless, Possible.* Shackleton tossed
an eager letter from "three sporty girls" into another.

Also selected from the *Possible* file was this tall
schoolmaster and freshly ordained minister,
Spencer-Smith, naval petty officer Ernest Wild,
and John Cope, a biology student who added
four years to his age to improve his chances.

The clatter of the morning crowds, rumbling
carts, vendors hawking war headlines; the screech
and hiss of locomotives, their monstrous chuffs,
billows of steam; whistles, wailing babies,
reverberating announcements. All the hubbub

dulls as Shackleton points to the huge station clock
and suggests they imagine Antarctica as that clock face.
His ship, the *Endurance*, will sail to the eleven o'clock
position and anchor there in the Weddell Sea.

He and five men will sledge toward the center,
to the pole, then on to the Ross Sea,
at the six o'clock.

The Ross Sea party gazes at the large six
where they're bound, sailing on the *Aurora*.
Their job will be to sledge inland, laying a line
of supply depots crucial to Shackleton's survival.

The long hand ticks away the moment.

A round of hearty handshakes and Shackleton
looks squarely to Cope, to Ernest Wild, to Hayward
and Spencer-Smith, and finally to Joseph Stenhouse,
who will serve as first officer on the *Aurora*.

Galvanized, the group straightens.
He lifts his chin and offers them all a crisp nod.

Dear Father,

You'll be surprised to hear from me as by this time we should have been at sea. There were maddening delays in Sydney. Captain Mackintosh was shorted in the funding, and we've had to scramble. He's furious with London, and, because of the lack of promised equipment and stores, we've had to beg donations and borrow equipment. Mackintosh asked the crew to defer their wages.

Fortunately, he and I get on well. He's a fine Scot and was with Shackleton on the *Nimrod* so knows the Antarctic. Frank Wild told me that was when Mack lost his right eye to a cargo hook. His chances for a bid to the South Pole were ruined then so you can imagine he's eager about this assignment.

I've seen to refitting the *Aurora*. She was in a sorry state. It's fortunate I'm a shipbuilder's son. Sailing her into Hobart I could see she's a roller—an old Dundee-built whaler—oak and greenheart timbered, fir lined with a steel-plated hull. The old girl's withstood pack ice several times.

Wild's brother, Ernest, is with us. He has charge of the dogs. You can't imagine what a job it is to crate and stow them. What a snarling tangle!

Leaving London, we saw warships everywhere. I haven't spared a minute to think about war. That we were granted permission to proceed tells me they don't expect the war will last long.

It weighs on us that we cannot contact the *Endurance* and alert them we're a month behind schedule. Our delay meant Mackintosh got the telegram saying he's had his second daughter born. We'll claim that as a good omen.

Have a happy Christmas. I will think of you all on Hogmanay when we'll sing "Auld Lang Syne." Imagine, by the time you get this letter, we'll have reached Antarctica!

Sincerest love to you all,
Joseph

Southing

The Reverend Arnold Spencer-Smith

Mack wears a gold glass for his one good eye
and has a splendid gentleman's manner.
Our ship needed overhaul and supplies
which delayed us a month—threw a spanner
in the schedule, but Mack sorted it out.
I was pleased when he asked me to say grace
at meals, and though most of the men aren't devout,
that may change if a man has death to face.
The wife of Tasmania's governor
gave Mack a fine portrait of Captain Scott.
That heroic man had been her brother.
I took a snap and in that moment caught
the commander's shudder, 'though he conveyed
his thanks. Next morning, we were underway.

Aeneas Lionel Acton Mackintosh

Thank God we're refitted and underway,
heading south at last. We've had our Christmas.
A proper feast. All my thoughts on that day
were of home, of wee Pamela, Gladys,
and our newborn lassie, who I won't know
before she's two. And because Gladys asked,
I've promised: This will be my last wallow.
The *Aurora* rolls, but she holds steadfast
in these frenzied seas. *Full sail on!* We've lost
time, a full month delayed. I feel my blood
racing too, as the ordinary, soft
life falls far behind. For all those I love,
for these men, and The Boss, I'm duty-bound.
Whatever comes, I will not let them down.

Victor George Hayward

Whatever I eat I cannot keep it down.
The dogs are sick too. We've had rough weather.
Enormous waves. I'll be ill 'til I've found
my sea legs. Mack gave us embossed leather
journals. I've fixed your dear portrait inside.
These are fine fellows. Wild jokes that in name
and in nature, he's wild. He provides
a good laugh. Old Joyce is our self-proclaimed
sledging expert. Last night, he recited
a poem called "The Cremation of Sam
McGee" which was jolly and delighted
us all. In quiet hours, though, I dream
of you and our wedding. When I come back,
we'll plan. I have absolute faith in Mack.

8

Ernest Edward Joyce

He makes plans, but I've more doubt than faith Mack
understands all we're up against. I hear
Stenhouse complained again. He wants me sacked.
I have a right, if they don't interfere,
to my jollifications, and Mack knows
I pull my pound. He needs this old penguin
and, besides which, it was *Shackleton* chose
me, put *me* in charge of sledging. We've one
wide-eyed London clerk, a young Aussie maths
teacher, and a tall twig from Queen's College
for clergy. The ship's surgeon, Cope—he lacks
a medical degree. Mack's acknowledged
my skills with sledging dogs. We've a green crew.
Hardship's ahead. It's me who'll get them through.

Harry Ernest Wild

A bit hard to sail a damned barnyard through
these swells. We've ducks, wet chickens, bawling sheep,
and twenty-six vicious dogs who came to
us without name tags. We have tried to keep
them sorted, but it's general mayhem, though
that clerk, Hayward, is keen; swapped out his spats
and flannels to help. He's handled dogs, shows
well for himself when they try to attack.
Kindness doesn't work on the dogs at all.
The ship's been taking on sea. There are times
she tried to stand on her head in a squall,
but she's a tough old girl. We look for signs
(orca and icebergs) that we're getting near.
Conditions aboard are rather severe.

Richard Walters Richards

The weather conditions have been severe,
but I signed on for a great adventure,
more than glad to end my teaching tenure.
Whilst I could have done my bit, volunteered
to join the fight, by all accounts it appeared
the war would end before I could enter
so I'm on this relic of a whaler
dangling over the side to pole ice clear
of the propeller. We weave through the pack,
the ship's steel-plated prow nosing the floes
apart. Ice hisses, groans in swells as Mack
finds a lane, prods forward. Progress is slow
in this ghostly fog. The wind's fallen slack.
The sails were iced so they've been furled and stowed.

Joseph Russel Stenhouse

The sails were iced stiff as metal. We've stowed
away seal meat for the dogs. One has died,
the rest are wretched. Steady gales have slowed
us. Slaughtered the sheep. Their carcasses ride
in the rigging and swing as the ship sways.
Joyce is troubled by the dogs' condition.
The skipper is haunted by our delays.
The ship's crew understands my commission
to be second in command, although back
before we left the merchant marine office,
I was assigned as ship's master, not Mack.
The officials there insisted, cautious
of his impairment. We Scots don't comply.
Mack's the skipper despite his one glass eye.

Penguins and Whales

Victor Hayward, January 1915

We've entered the Ross Sea.
This morning the captain was fair excited
thinking we'd found a piece of land
unmarked on the sea charts.
It was an iceberg five miles long.

There are whales in the water lanes,
whales everywhere. Hundreds.
Big groups of them circle near.

If only I could show you
a great blue whale, Ethel.
As it comes to the surface, it's a Goliath,
like an island rising to life.
Spencer-Smith tried for a photograph,
but the blue whale sounded, slowly
pouring its great body down to the deeps.
I stood a good while after
thinking it was a dream.

You'd laugh to see penguins!
They glide in the water, elegant and swift,
then pop nimble as Jack-be-quick
back onto ice and wobble around like ten pins.

Seals beyond counting loll on the floes—
lazy gray sausages with puppy eyes.
I made a sketch for you.

I watched a skua bird attack a shearwater
for its squid. It landed on the other bird's head,
biting, batting it with his wings,
until he could pirate away the prize.

Just now, we're sailing by an iceberg that's all-over
green, glowing like polished jade.
The sky is changing from rose to violet and orange
and, oh—someone's put Caruso on the gramophone.
I haven't words to describe this.
Even old Joyce and Mack stand together, staring.

THE SLEDGING COMMENCES

January–April 1915

Unknown to the Ross Sea party and the rest of the world, Shackleton's ship, the *Endurance*, is beset in pack ice.

I step into air cold and awash.
It feels like it is ringing, like it can nothing but ring.
It feels like astonishment.
I glance up and it is as though I have just been born.
   —RACHEL DILWORTH, "The Heart of the Matter"

Iceberg, Departing

Unbound, floating
through shrouds of mist and fog

out to the dark sea, I become my own landscape
     singular   pure
my own planet with one mineral—ice.

Like ice in the rings of Saturn
I circle in the current, play with light,
     dazzle it back to the sun.

Opal, moonstone, aquamarine, luminous as a ghost

I am learning storms, wind, blue whale lamentations,
the natter and chat of fluttery things,
     what it is to be suspended, rocked.

Such peacefulness, drifting
     cradled
in this warmth which tastes of salt.

The Sledging Commences

after "This Is Just to Say" by William Carlos Williams

Ernest Joyce, January 24, 1915

In his great rush, Mack's risking our dogs, that I
know are unfit, and the men's lives, as none have
any sledging experience. So, after we'd eaten
yesterday, I gave the team a serious talk on the
blisters that freeze in their hands like black plums,
about snow blindness and scurvy, frostbite that
goes gangrene. They all know of men who were
here before and died, who starved and froze in
their tents. I told 'em it's my seventh journey to the
Minna Bluff, and I'd see them through this icebox.

Mack's also decided to winter the *Aurora* here, and
it's damned foolish rot. I say, send her north, which
means she won't be iced in or worse! But you
don't argue with the skipper. Then, after we were
all asleep, a few dogs got free and fought, probably
due to their wolf strain. One was hurt beyond saving.
I've insisted we be exact about packing supplies for
ourselves into bags which each hold a breakfast,

lunch, and dinner for three men. No one will forgive
a mistake when he's done in and cold. It's down to me
to figure out each sledge's load careful so that they
carry all required but can still be hauled. And, if it were
needed, they'll eat seals and decide they're delicious,
by God, when they're hungry. It's come time now, so
we gather 'round and raise the toast to wives and sweet-
hearts, and that they never meet. Three of us men and
seven dogs harness up, and the others cheer, call out, *So
long! Good luck!* Then we bend hard into the wind and cold.

Relaying the Load

Ernest Wild, February 1, 1915

We slog toward the barrier in thigh-deep snow.
Over a thousand pounds are loaded on our sledge.
In harness, a team of bone-tired men and dogs.
Mack takes a bearing and estimates distance.

There's no going on with this load on our sledge
so we decide to relay. Mack hollers, whips the dogs.
He takes another bearing, reads the distance.
We unload half the load, haul forty yards forward, return

to relay the second half. Mack beats the dogs.
I fall a long way down a small crevasse.
We haul half the load forty yards more, unload, return.
Repeat. In two hours, we advance a hundred yards.

Mack sinks to his shoulders in a crevasse.
We heave and heave just to get the runners started.
Repeat. In eight hours, we gain four hundred yards.
Mack's hands fester with sores. My toes are going.

We heave and heave knowing that this job's just started
and already we're a team of bone-tired men and dogs.
Mack's hands fester with sores. My feet are numb.
We slog up the barrier in thigh-deep snow.

The Race to Minna Bluff

Ernest Joyce, February 1915

Seven miles in three days, but, by God,
we're up on the barrier now and moving.
Mack's promised a magnum of champagne
for the team to reach the bluff first. His joke.
We've a routine. The three of us travel by day;
Mack's team passes us by night as we rest.
Yesterday, Wild left us another message
in the snow. It read: *Pub Ahead.*

Today we found Jock, Mack's lead dog
tethered to a pole with some seal meat
and a snow shelter. I suppose Mack intended
to pick him up in a few weeks on his way
back. I see he's been knocking the hell
out of him. Mack hasn't any damned idea
how to manage dogs. I harnessed
Jock up, and he pulls splendidly for us.

The temperature's dropped. It's bitter
cold but smoother for sledging. Every mile
and a half we stop and build a snow cairn
to mark our way back. The barrier's vast
as a frozen sea. Sometimes there's ice waves,
tall peaks of sastrugi we battle up time
and again. There's a strange stillness
on the barrier, a quiet broken only by

the shush of our runners. We march on,
lost in our own thoughts. Mack and Smithy
quote plummy poets, but no one puts it
better than Robert Service—he lived
a time in the Yukon and so he knew

the white land locked tight as a drum,
the cold fear that follows and finds you,
the silence that bludgeons you dumb.

Last Night I Slept Like a Top

Ernest Wild, February 1915

Wedged in my frozen sleeping bag,
the tent walls chattering,
my every breath caused ice to drip.
I settled myself thinking of sailing.

Joyce lashed bamboo masts
at the front of the sledges to hang
gear at the ready—binoculars, fur mitts,
the prismatic compass.

Yesterday we had a favorable wind,
so he fastened a snow cloth
to our mast and, for a bit, the sledge
skimmed the hard crust, runners flying
and dogs racing, all of us ripping along.

Everything sparkled. The air, the snow.
The sun arced halos, splendid shining
rings with twin sundogs.

Struck by the majesty of it all
I opened my mouth to whoop
into the wind and every iced hair
on my face near tore from the root.

79° South, Minna Bluff Depot

The Rev. Spencer-Smith, February 11, 1915

I have built a cairn and a grave marker
for yet another dog. Bobs died. Mack's

reorganized teams for his departure
with Wild and Joyce. I'm to return back

north to Hut Point with two men, our supplies,
and four of the dogs, near dead on their feet.

In spite of everything that Joyce advised,
Mack will not stop 'til this job is complete.

Even though it's unlikely Shackleton
will cross this year, Mack's going further south.

I pray for Wild, Joyce, and our captain,
who says even if Shack's crossing's in doubt

he must go on or have himself to blame.
I quite see his point. It's all in the game.

A Glimpse of Hell

Dodging about the Sound, avoiding and clearing floes and growlers in heavy drift when we could see nothing, our compass unreliable . . . I had a glimpse of Hell.

—JOSEPH STENHOUSE

On the *Aurora*, February 21–24, 1915

By God, she's proved her worth. We'd been keeping
the *Aurora* on the move, searching out a stable place
to berth, but the land was shrouded in mist. Visibility
no more than one hundred yards. I had no idea
what water was beneath us.

High seas running. Heavy growlers and floes.
We were on the watch around the clock, anchoring
to ice, but the wind kept breaking us free.
We finally secured to the north side of the Glacier Tongue
on February 21. Three days later, violent winds

jammed her broadside to the wall of ice.
The rudder post ground against it. I feared a great slab
of ice might fall away and crush us. For six hours,
the ship was slammed and battered.

Then, the winds shifted. We made our escape
to Cape Evans, and now we've twenty-three fathoms
beneath her. We keep close watch on passing bergs.
Mackintosh said the sledging parties would return
to Hut Point by March 20 and look for us to come.

I'll risk the ship no further. Mack knows she's our one
ticket home. We'll wait here, hope the sound solidifies,
and see the old girl tended to. I've ordered the crew
to build a raft, carry stern anchors to shore. We'll bury
the anchors and prepare to winter here.

Dead Dog Trail

> The men of the Ross Sea party hauled a load averaging 300–335
> pounds each. They had no idea the weight was unprecedented.
> —KELLY TYLER-LEWIS, *The Lost Men*

March 2, 1915

Wild names it, haunted by
the rise and fall of howls
bleeding outward in limitless
white at the bottom of the earth,

sound ancient as a sacred bell
or thin mountain air
keening through the ruined stones
and skulls of a vanished race,

the hollow bone song of the near dead.

One by one, the nine dogs perish.
Pinkey is last. She rode for a time
on the sledge with Wild, whose feet
are foot-shaped lumps of raw meat.

Mack, Wild, and Joyce manage five miles
every ten hours. Finally, they lay Shackleton's
depot at 80° S and turn back for Hut Point,
one hundred sixty miles to the north.

They have provisions to last one week.

Waiting for Deliverance

The Rev. Spencer-Smith, Discovery Hut, March 1915

Had a fine meal when our team first arrived.
Our two dogs, Towser and Gunner, were near dead,

though now, in this barren hut we survive
the weeks on less and less. But, as I've said,

we thank our Father for our safe return,
for this shelter and our lives. Amen.

As the weeks have crept by our main concern
is for Mack, Joyce, and Wild, the last men

still out on the ice. Here, the food's quite low.
Three nights ago, I sent up our last flare.

The bright sparks showered down, died on the snow.
But, look now! Glory! The *Aurora*'s here,

ghosting through the sea fog. We climb aboard
to eat, wash, have a smoke, and are restored.

23

Iced In

Joseph Stenhouse, March 1915

Another gale. This one rocked the ship
until the anchors gave way, and we were
heeled over, spindrift and snow blinding us.
We managed to sail to Hut Point and pick up
the four smoke-blackened scarecrows
waiting there and land supplies for the last
sledgers still out on the ice.

The gale threatened to rip away her masts
and spars, but the *Aurora* labored on. Spray
froze to the rigging, ice coated the rolling decks.
Three times I was sure icebergs would take us.
On March 14, we worked the vessel back.
We ran the wires and cables to anchor in,
and by the 23, the sound congealed solid.

Spencer-Smith, Richards, and the two scientists
were all queasy, but got tidied up and are glad
for their tobacco. They're now busy fitting out
the Cape Evans Hut as a scientific station,
coming and going to the ship for meals and supplies.
Their tales of depot laying leave me most anxious
to see Commander Mackintosh and the other five safe.

Spencer-Smith's Woodbines

[*an erasure of "Cigarettes" by B. H. Fairchild*]

The bloom of nicotine puts me right—
the minute flares in the deep dark,
in hands telling stories. Drowsy voices.

Bad news craves cigarettes.
I've seen grief let smoke gather slowly,
rise and rise, unravel in frayed strands.

Cigarettes make bleakness nutritional, or at least useful.
They tell us the work is done, done well;
    whisper
        yes, yes, oh yes.

Frostbite, Last Team on the Barrier

Ernest Wild, March 24, 1915

On half rations, we headed to safety camp
fifty miles north. Day after day, small steps.
By the time we got there, I could barely limp.
We were down to crumbs and cocoa.

After a night and feed from the stores
at safety camp, we managed to go on,
me hobbling. Frostbite was worse. By the end
of that day, we made the barrier's edge.

Played out, Mack and Joyce dumped the sledge,
tent, sleeping bags, and gear and unencumbered
we risked sliding down the ice slopes
on our backsides, then gimped into Hut Point

where Cope, Hayward, and Jack fed and thawed us.
Cope removed my port lug and a starboard toe,
as both ear and toe were dead and gone entire.
Likely my looks are greatly improved.

LEARNING DETACHMENT

April 1915–August 1915

APRIL 22. In Ypres, Belgium, German troops fire more than one hundred fifty tons of chlorine gas along four miles of the front, marking the first large-scale use of poison gas.

MAY 1. The sun disappears from Antarctica for four months of winter. The *Endurance* continues to drift northward, trapped in ice. Shackleton and his men live aboard waiting for the Antarctic summer to release them.

without sun, stars or moon
but a peculiar light as of thought

that spins a dark fire—
whirling upon itself until,
in the cold, it kindles

to make a man aware of nothing
that he knows . . .
—WILLIAM CARLOS WILLIAMS, "There"

Learning Detachment

Antarctica

I think of the small one,
India, when the night is so black it pulls
outward, like a riptide.
Her shape once nestled warm against me.

We jostled like pack ice, bumped
and then drifted apart.
Africa's great muscular body embraced
South America until they broke up.
Australia simply rafted off.

There is no language for what I want.
I do not long for them, but something
calls me, out there in the night.

In the dark, the whole crevasse
of space glinting, it helps to remember
how South America lingered,

her peninsula locked
fingertip to fingertip with mine,
holding on, until bit by bit, we slipped
and, cold and alone, I fell away.

Sea Wolves

Victor Hayward, April 1915

It's taboo to speculate about why the *Aurora*
hasn't come for us. Mack's weary of our bickering,
and the gloom in this hut puts us out of sorts.

For light, we rely on a bit of canvas afloat in a tin
of blubber. There are no chairs, tables, or beds.
We have three bags for the six of us, so sleep in turns.

Stenhouse landed enough stores to exist awhile,
and everyone's bandaged up, but the idleness
and smoke grow tiresome.

Mack calls the filth insufferable, says we live
like troglodytes eating with our dirty hands. I twisted
wire into crude utensils, but soot covered and greasy,
with matted hair, tangled beards, we do look savage.

Often, Mack and I leave the hut to inspect the sound,
see if the ice is solid enough to cross the thirteen
miles to reach the ship.

Today, the ice is eight inches thick, but there are wide
water lanes between the floes made by killer whales.
They break the ice easily, sporting about.

Mack and I watch four whales hunt a seal
resting on a large floe: one whale nudges the ice,
turns it into position, and by some signal,
the pack charges the floe together then dives
beneath it. They smash their tails, making a wave.

29

The floe rocks, the seal clings on, scrambles for purchase
on its slippery island but—by Jingo! The wave tilts
the floe and the seal slides into teeth waiting in the sea.

The Lay of the Land

Hut Point, April 1915

Suppose your right hand is Ross Island,
just off the southern coast of Antarctica.
In your palm lies Mount Erebus. Its black

smoke roils up, clouds reflect the volcano's
scarlet core. Imagine now that your fingers
point south to Antarctica's cold heart.

Your forefinger nudges the Ross Ice Barrier,
a sheet of ice the size of France
you've sledged for three full months.

Between your thumb and forefinger
are the treacherous waters of McMurdo Sound
where you believe the *Aurora* is anchored

but should have come for you by now
with all its comforts: clean bunk, fresh clothes,
soap, coal to heat water, proper food.

Hut Point is the tip of your forefinger, where
you're hunkered in an eight by fifteen-foot section
of a snow-filled storage shack Scott named

Discovery Hut. On the same island, thirteen miles
north, at the meaty base of your thumb
is the Cape Evans hut. The others are there

and near enough to eat and bathe on the ship.
One route to Cape Evans is over steep, iced ground
and blocked by a glacier tongue riddled

with crevasses. Or you might cross the sound
but only after it solidifies, or the ice floes
and you with them will be blown out to sea

by katabatic winds roaring down the mountain,
and the ice must be thick enough whales
won't break and lift it to reach you.

You stare at your filthy hand, blistered, bandaged,
knowing it will be at least another month
before it's washed in anything other than seal blood.

Gladys Mackintosh

Bedford, England, April 1915

Your face comes to me and goes like breath on a mirror.
It's a milky morning. The baby dozes. We all miss you.

Our chiffchaffs have returned, such cheery singers.
Your face comes to me and goes like breath on a mirror.

She's such a good baby. I so wish you could see her
sleeping now or hear her laugh and coo.

Your face comes to me and goes like breath on a mirror.
It's a milky morning. The baby dozes. Where are you?

Wild's Hut Point Mixture

> If only a case of tobacco had been landed. A pipe of this
> soothing weed makes all the world akin.
> —ERNEST JOYCE

Desperate for tobacco,
Joyce tamped shreds
of dehydrated vegetables,
into his pipe, bit down
and got the mess smoking
until a general outcry roared up
and we begged him to stop.

I experimented a bit
and found the perfect blend
of tea leaves, coffee grounds,
sawdust, and sennegrass
to be a fine substitute.
It survived all criticism
once I added a few dried herbs.

Butchering Seals in the Dark

Hut Point, April 1915

Hayward kneels in blood-blackened snow
and greasy gore of seal carcasses,
warming his hands in the entrails,

and gazes into the Antarctic night.
A green glow ruffles and billows, shifts
in the shine on the ice,

and this otherworldly light
enters Hayward's mind as music,
far and faint, a melody

Ethel once hummed into his chest
as he held her, folded to him, dancing.
Hayward closes his eyes and sways,

sickened by his blood-matted beard
and hair, the blubber stench, the squalid hut,
by the impassible distance between the hut

and comfort of Cape Evans, between
Antarctica and a way home,
between himself and the man he once was.

Fell in the Pond

Ernest Wild, May 1915

Joyce and I were out testing the ice,
and down I went up to my waist
in a seal hole. It was 50 below
and I made tracks fast as I could
back to the hut. Hayward lent me

pants but Mack wouldn't lend me
his combination suit to wear
till I got my clothes dried out.
He said it was frozen, but it's not.
I saw it dry as a bone in his bag.

I cannot understand Mack at all.
He didn't offer me the sleeping bag
we take turns with, me shaking
and dripping. He just rolled over
and went on snoring.

Yesterday he said he thought he
might make a dash to Cape Evans,
take one of us along, but no gear—
just nip across, light. Sheer daftness!
He says if a blizzard pops up, he'll lie

down, cover over with his Burberry.
It's one more of his mad schemes.
To my way of thinking, he's just after
the comforts of his cabin on the ship
and is done mixing with the lower ranks.

The Red Comet

Your first and paramount duty will be to look after the safety of
the ship, this comes before everything else.
—MACKINTOSH TO STENHOUSE

Joseph Stenhouse, May 6, 1915

We've shackled the *Aurora* to solid land
with seven steel hawsers paid out
to anchors biting deep into frozen gravel.

Our heaviest two anchors have been dropped
seventy fathoms down to grip the seabed.
My boatswain says the moorings would hold

a battleship. We adjust the cables daily till
they twang and quiver, taut as fiddle-strings.
The rum's low, and the crew's quarrelsome.

Their nerves are raw. The ink in my pen
is frozen. In all, we haven't had a rosy time
finding a good place to winter the ship.

Once the ice in the sound finally congealed
and locked us in, I ordered the boiler drawn
down and the engines made ready for repairs.

Four nights ago, a red comet sliced over
Mount Erebus. Its tail made a long white scar
on the dark. The crew think it was an omen.

Today, we heard a deep rumble come from
Erebus. Its white plume spewed much higher
from the volcano's core. Nothing more until

tonight, when the sea began to swell and roll
beneath the ice. Now, wires thrum, the chains
strain, and the wind's blustered into a gale.

The cables sing, crescendo like sopranos
attempting to shatter glass. Into this ungodly din
comes a tremendous *crack!* and a cable zings

across the deck like a blade. Another—*crack!*
The report like a rifle shot and a second line's gone.
Then, of a sudden, one massive slab of ice breaks

with a hellish roar. The ship lurches, swings.
Ice slams its weight against her timbers,
battering, and there's Paton, the boatswain,

running with a lantern, yelling, *She's away
wi'it!* which any ass can see. I order steam
on the main engines, but they're dismantled,

which I know full well, so I set the men
to relieving the tackles on the cables so
the anchors won't drag and topple the ship.

Violent wind, black waves roiling.
We're caught, beset, and we drift away.
Masses of ice ram us northwest,

and when I can raise my head a moment,
there go the lit windows of the Cape Evans hut
disappearing in whirling snow.

Cape Evans Hut

The Rev. Spencer-Smith, May 6, 1915

We've all the luxuries the ship affords
as we trek the ice back and forth, ship

to Cape Evans hut. We're keeping records
of scientific studies, making trips

to hunt seals, observe penguins, log weather
data. We play bridge, putter about, chat,

argue in a friendly way together.
We are all in general agreement that

the war can't still be going on. Richards,
out checking wind instruments this morning,

was stunned to his core when he looked seaward
and saw the *Aurora's* snapped her moorings,

left the steel-cabled hawsers frayed like string.
Our ship's been swept away. With everything.

Midwinter's Day, Cape Evans

Ernest Wild, June 1915

Plum pudding and tobacco, potted beef tongue
and songs. Prizes for relay race winners.

We found a bounty of flour and jam, lovely
bottled fruits left years before by Scott.
Then, like Christmas, Gaze produced
a bottle of scotch.

It's an improvement over life at Hut Point
as here there's soap and a tub, gas lights,
a cast-iron range and insulated walls, mattresses
and bunks, a laboratory, a darkroom for the Padre,
and an outdoor latrine.

We play at cards and read. I've a mystery book.
Already there's been a murder and I expect
several more. A full set of *Encyclopedia Britannica*
was off-loaded before the *Aurora* disappeared,
so we can settle our arguments proper.

We've only the clothes on our backs,
so from my little sewing shop, Joyce in my employ,
we'll stitch up the most excellent trousers
a man could want, trousers for the whole company
cut from Scott's old, ruined tents,
the finest canvas on the continent.

Curled outdoors are the five dogs we've got left.
They're kept well apart as they'd be pleased
to kill each other. The one female, Bitchy, is pregnant.

Richards buries himself in things meteorological,
and Hayward hunts seals for the Padre to cook up.

Today, Mack says we can poke a bit into the Tru-milk
and Nut Food saved up for sledging rations,
the skipper's that sure the *Aurora* will withstand
the ice and be back for us by summer.

We'll Do Our Damnedest

Victor Hayward, Cape Evans, July 1915

Sprained my wrist yesterday.
Gaze and I hit a rock tobogganing,
and we stove in the sledge. Gaze
is worse for it. He ricked his ankle
and lost a piece of his nose.

I've been reading *Lorna Doone*.
You must read it, Ethel.
It expresses so much that I feel.

I spend time planning our Cricklewood
house. Don't you think a holiday cottage
in the Broads a fine idea? We'll hire
a yacht and sail at least as far as Martham.

I've heard there's a strange marker
at Martham's church inscribed *My mother
was my sister, my mistress, and my wife.*

Mack reviewed sledging arrangements
and allowed every man to voice his opinion.
By the first of September, we're to shift
4000 pounds of stores to Safety Camp
on the barrier, twenty-three miles away.

Beginning October, we'll make four trips
to Minna Bluff, 100 miles south, then parties
will be arranged to build supply depots
at 80°, 81°, 82°, 83°, finishing with one
at Mount Hope. Mack has it all worked out.

It's a stupendous undertaking and will be hard going for five months but, in the end, we should be back by March. The skipper said that if we can accomplish this, it will be almost a record of South Polar travel. *Deo Volente*, the Padre says.

Beyond the Narwhal Gate

> And the blind eye creates
> the empty forms between the ivory gates
> —T. S. ELIOT, "Ash-Wednesday"

Cape Evans, Antarctic Winter 1915

Aeneas Mackintosh settles onto Capt. Scott's
   old bed wishing again for the services

   of an intermediary, a first officer
who would call the men into line.

He removes his glass eye, shuts and shelves
   its leather box and falls into a dream

of glittering ice, the teeth in a crevasse's gullet.

   Aeneas descends

dropping through sapphire, through cobalt, down
   and down to the indigo netherworld.

❉

   An earthy stench. Decay. The scent
of burnt blubber
     conjures India,
the plantation where he was born.

   Blistering heat. Scythes.

Blue-limbed men waist deep in great vats,
   beat and stir, froth green water into blue.

Women with blue-black hair and larkspur hands
    hoist sodden sheaves
from the steeping tanks, cut indigo into cakes.

Silhouetted by glare, his father, seated high
    on a horse, points a riding crop

to an immense gate made of narwhal tusks,
    a colossal archway.

Remember who you are named for.

Stunning brightness dissolves
    to shifting scrims of snow.

❄

Beyond the narwhal gate, distant figures loom
    familiar to his mind—

how many? Six? Three? Yes, three
falter forward, stumble, fall in the snow.

    Aeneas lurches toward them,
his legs plowing powdery drifts,

drifts rising to calf, now thigh,
    now hip deep. He fights on, knowing

this is fated. Shackleton is coming,
    and Aeneas will save him.

Two Hundred Fifty Miles Out, Nine Day Coal Supply

Joseph Stenhouse, July 1915

We are eighteen men locked in ice.
In their bunks, the crew are exhausted
by the cold and nerves.

Quiet tonight. Pack ice mutes the waves.
The ship creaks.
I watch the sea ice, bright in moonlight,

and the weight of night falls down upon me
like a heap of fishing net.
My old curse has returned, the blackness
that shadows my mind.

Six nights ago, we were very near abandoning
the ship. The men had stuffed their pillowcases
with their possessions.

Floes collided, climbed the backs of other slabs,
steepled into ridges fifteen feet high.

The *Aurora* was spun like a compass needle
and wedged between two walls of ice.
Her timbers screeched from the pressure.

At the railings, we watched in horror as her oak
and iron five-ton rudder was wrenched to starboard
and smashed to splinters.

By that evening, a gale forced the men below.
They ate in silence then went to their bunks.

I told them to keep doors ajar as pressure
was skewing the frames. If they jammed shut
and the ship sunk, they'd be trapped.

I could see the midship was hogging,
the *Aurora*'s keel bending like a twig.
Ice pinched her bow and stern

the way one might absently press two ends
of a playing card into an arch.
I feared her spine would be broken.

We poured battery acid on the ice
around her stern-post. Futile.
Time and again the ship was concertinaed

until suddenly the bow jerked sidewise
and jacked high on a floe. The keel crashed down
and free. Sprung!

Her prow was still breached but the stern
floated in a patch of water.
The crew wept like girls.

Now, we drift on, spared.
I keep the men busy and the blackness
stowed beneath an untroubled face.

THE GOLDEN GATEWAY

September 1915–February 1916

NOVEMBER 21, 1915. Ernest Shackleton's ship, the *Endurance*, sinks hundreds of miles from land in the Weddell Sea. His party never sets foot on Antarctica.

If you came this way,
Taking any route, starting from anywhere,
At any time or at any season,
It would always be the same: you would have to put off
Sense and notion. You are not here to verify,
Instruct yourself, or inform curiosity
Or carry report. You are here to kneel.

     —T. S. ELIOT, "Little Gidding"

All My Flowers

Antarctica

I know ice whalebone white
    green and turquoise,

    milky ice, ice blood-red
when the algae blooms; candle ice, pack ice,

    pancake ice, and cat ice that glazes
water so thinly a breath would shatter it;
       lolly slush,

loose crystals in a salt-water slurry;
    young ice and its false maturity.
I know the way fast ice locks on

       and doesn't let go;
the gray moiré of grease ice, its sheen
of watermarked silk skimming the sea;

and fog ice, mists of diamond dust
     that cancel skies, that conjure
multiple and dazzling suns,

bounce prisms, throw halos,
    suspend a snow field, inverted, in midair.

❄

    The ice gives birth to ice.
The first filaments of ice mating are frazil ice.

Once it develops and grows muscular
    ice battles ice.

The ice barrage explodes
in a din of booms, cannonades, cracks loud as rifle shots.

And when the ice buries ice
it is entombed with ancient atmospheres.

All my hours are ice hours.
　　All my flowers are ice flowers.

After Four Months, Dawn

First, the perpetual gloaming—
greens and purples bruise the sky.

Then, reds, the hard orange glow;
smoke haze from a hundred forest fires,
the blaze of a hundred battlefields.

At last, from behind the mountains,
the suite of colors bursts, delivers
the galvanizing, golden sun

and we stand mute on the ice
as this holy thing is born.

Parting Company on the Barrier

Ernest Joyce, October 12, 1915

Mack needs to study the men.
They're putting their hearts to it
but can't keep it up. He only thinks

about Shackleton's party coming.
We're trying to pull two hundred
pounds apiece in heavy drift,

and he won't use the dogs!
Mack's too damned pigheaded
to see his plan is the worst

kind of foolishness. Our first day
it took five hours of agony
to advance a mile.

I told him flat he was mad.
Wasted an hour this morning,
arguing. In the end,

he pushed on with the Padre
and Wild after dumping
sixty pounds from their sledge

on us. We're left to shift 1,392
pounds of stores to the Bluff
on two sledges. Very well.

I've a new plan: we'll relay
the loads with one extra trip
to the Bluff and reroute to trim

some miles. We'll have to steer
through crevasses but my party's
keen. I won't give odds on Mack's.

Rudderless

Joseph Stenhouse, October 1915

The cook and boatswain slept
in frosted grottoes until the sun
returned to us. Every exhaled
breath froze to their cabin walls.

My own berth has a stove
but there's a penalty for warmth.
The stoves belch sulfur fumes.
Often, I woke retching and dizzy.
The men had to drag me twice
from my bed, unconscious,
but now things are running smoothly
aboard. Work is a tonic.

It was −20° when we dug away
the ice and snow to begin
the back-breaking job of removing
our damaged rudder from the stern.
After two long days, we dropped it
onto the floe behind us.

We are busy now rigging a jury rudder,
from salvaged ironwork, timbers,
concrete mixed with boiling water.
Without it we will never manage
to steer back to the sound. It is torment
to think of the men left at Cape Evans.

My crew is in fine fettle, although
today I nearly took Larkman's head off
having a go at his bad tooth.
I gave two great heaves without success.

He was near a swoon before I stopped.
Larkman was a brick to bear it.

The men play cricket on the ice.
Evenings, whist and chess.
From the crow's nest, I watch floes split
into lanes, congeal, then divide again.
Vapors rise like smoke from the open water.
It is strangely beautiful in moonlight.

Snow-Blind, 79° S, Replenishing Supply Depots

Victor Hayward, November 1915

New snow, fine as flour billowing
from mother's bread bowl. (Wish I'd
not thought of her bread.) It's hard going.
The dogs wallow, sink to their bellies.
They whine and bury their heads in snow
to relieve their burning eyes. I stagger
alongside the sledge, useless, snow-blind.
My eyes and nose run, then it all
freezes in my beard. I cannot imagine,
Ethel, what you would think to see me.

The constant sun sears even with goggles.
Joyce uses a leather strap with a slit
for his eyes. He packed cocaine slivers
under his lids and mine. Even Mack's bone
socket burns without his glass eye.
I try to dream about our picnics, plans
made in the leafy park. I want to smell grass,
your hair, hear a blackcap sing. If only
I could feel your sweet hand on my face.
O love, what am I doing here?

Summer Begins, on the Aurora

Joseph Stenhouse, November 21, 1915

Sea smoke. Fog. Leaden
days without depth or border.

We creak along
locked in the torpid pace
of the pack ice.

After six and a half months,
we're conveyed across
the Antarctic Circle.

I watch floes fracture apart
then reseal in the randomness
of wind and current.

No sea lanes open
worth spending the coal.
Snow's melting in the scuppers.

Soon we'll know
where the old girl leaks.

Gladys Mackintosh, Advent

Bedford, England, December 1915

The garden's lovely now covered in fresh snow.
You'd laugh to see our Pamela making paper chains.

I found a waxwing. At the window, heard the blow.
In the garden, his lovely body shone lying in the snow
by the holly tree. You'd cheer me with a story. I know—

you'd say he was drunk on berries. Oh, to see you again
in the garden, Love. I imagine you'd clown in the snow
to coax a laugh from Pamela making paper chains.

Hogmanay, on the Aurora

Joseph Stenhouse, January 1, 1916

For Christmas Day,
I'd organized a feast for the men
from conserved stores.

Cigars. An extra tot.
Allowed Cook precious coal
to bake bread.

It all turned my stomach.
We stuffed ourselves
whilst at Cape Evans

those poor beggars
have nothing. I thanked God
when Christmas was over.

Now, a costumed fou-fou band
clatters out at midnight,
for Hogmanay

with a mouth organ
and marline spikes for triangles.
Grady stomps about

with a kerosene tin
strung on his neck for a drum.
Kavanagh stands smart

at attention and drowns out
everyone, earnestly banging away
on a packing case.

Paton hollers *Good New Year!*
and leads a lusty, if tuneless, rendition
of "God Save the King."

Much backslapping,
loud cheers and we toast to
a better year to come.

Black Flags to the Beardmore Glacier

Ernest Joyce, January 1916

Richy's feeding the dogs hot hoosh,
and it's a joy to see them relish their food.

Piled a tower of ice blocks at 81° S
twice as tall as the Padre.

Staked bamboo poles with four flags
on top to mark the supply depot.

Beneath are enough provisions and oil
to carry twelve men to 80° S.

As we go, every quarter hour,
we erect a cairn to guide our return
and show Shackleton the route.

It gives the dogs a spello and Smithy
gets a sit. Mack can rest his sprained knee.

Cocaine's low, but I saw the dogs
rub their faces in snow and a handful
over my eyes gives instant relief.

We're out of black bunting so I cut up
a set of Richy's soot-blackened trousers.

In this thick weather if we keep two flags
in a line behind us, we can steer forward.

Might be able to sight Mt. Hope
from fifty miles off though our chart

is old and Mt. Hope isn't marked.
Should get there in a fortnight.

The Golden Gateway, Final Depot 83° 31′ S

A glorious spectacle. A mighty silence.
—ERNEST JOYCE, January 26, 1916

Cragged mountains compress one hundred miles
of the Beardmore Glacier. Its ice buckles
into the deepest crevasses on Earth
where far below, in the blue-black cold,

are belly-drags of ancient beetles, imprints
of primeval tundra, tail tracings, meteorites
from Mars and Mercury, fragments
of stars born before, long before, our star.

The men stand amazed by scale, by sun-bronzed
granite, cobalt blue caves, a lavender sky
ribboned amber and orange. Particles of ice tinsel
air so dry, so crystalline, air seems entirely absent.

It's taken one hundred forty-eight days
to reach Mount Hope, the hill they are sure
they've found as two of Scott's abandoned
sledges lie half buried in the snow nearby.

They construct the last depot. Wild tucks in a letter
for his brother on the *Endurance* team, teasing likely,
that he'd arrived here before Frank. Hayward snaps
a photo of the three black flags atop the cairn.

They've done the near impossible.
With the help of good old Providence, Joyce says,
they'll make it back by the end of February.
They have three hundred sixty miles to travel.

Hayward massages methylated spirits into Mack's
swollen legs. Everyone's gums are black, Joyce is snow-

blind. *Next enterprise is the long trail back,* he thinks.
The dogs are our only hope. Our lives depend on them.

Richards makes a last scan of every tent-shaped
boulder. No sign of Shackleton. A bit of quartz
he's found sets him thinking of Australia and gold
mines at home in Bendigo.

Trapped Returning, the Twelve Day Blizzard

> As regards disaster, they each have their two tablets of
> morphia.
> —ERNEST SHACKLETON

February 22, 1916

For the fifth day, the blizzard claws their two tents
smaller, crushes their bodies tighter together.
Shrieks rise and rise, rattle ribs, quake the bowels,

then die back. Joyce hears Wild's tenor drift
from the other tent. *So they're in the land of the living,*
Joyce writes in his diary. Wild recorded: *Had two biscuits*

and a chunk of snow. Now, to comfort his tentmates,
he sings to Mack and the Padre, describes the pub he'll own,
imagines he'll tell this story while pulling a pint.

To escape his agonies, Spencer-Smith dreams
of *a pleasant afternoon in Gray's Inn,* of *Christmas*
candles, the organ crashing out bars of "Adeste Fideles."

Mackintosh writes nothing. All his pluck was sapped
shambling here. He lies in a pool of water,
reindeer hairs stuck to his face from the rotten bag.

The four dogs curl in a torpor beneath deep snow.
There's no food left for them. Joyce exhausts himself
digging out channels for the dogs to keep breathing.

Hayward sketches Ethel's profile in blue ink,
adds no other entry but the date and his mark for "ditto"
to the growing column beneath the word *Blizzard.*

Richards props up in his sodden bag next to Hayward
and Joyce to work the math again. He writes:
It would be very easy to die.

Morning. The storm slackens. Joyce bullies them
to dig out. The effort requires half the day;
they cannot shovel a minute without doubling over,

gasping. By late afternoon, they carry Spencer-Smith
from the tent, secure him in his bag on top of the sledge
loaded with equipment and the four men

and four dogs grind forward, Mack stumbling, roped
to the rear. They lurch through deep snow, blinded
and bent by the return of hurricane force winds.

After an hour, like log burnt through, Mack crumbles and falls.
I cannot go any further. Wrap me up in a deck cloth. Leave me.

Another calculation.

If they don't save the dogs, no one survives. Ten miles
to the Bluff Depot—if they can find it. Hayward, Joyce,
and Richards will go on. Wild will have to stay back

to keep Spencer-Smith and Mack alive. That evening,
Wild writes: *It is blizzarding worse. I hope to see them
in three- or four-days' time. I wonder if I'm right.*

And the Padre writes, *we had a great and glorious
cup of tea to warm us and sat up talking very late,
the wind still howling.*

67

WHITE EARTH AND RUINS

February–March 1916

FEBRUARY TO DECEMBER 1916. Britain suffers the two longest and bloodiest battles of World War I, at Verdun and the Somme.

These are the desolate, dark weeks
when nature in its barrenness
equals the stupidity of man.

The year plunges into night
and the heart plunges
lower than night

to an empty, windswept place
—WILLIAM CARLOS WILLIAMS, "There"

The Cold, Quiescent Eye

Antarctic Winter Solstice

In the still air
between the ice sheet
and clouds

diamond dust sifts down
and particle by particle
   adds to a weight

      so colossal
      it deforms the sphere of Earth.

There is a grief arid as this,
   antiseptic   numb

Airglow, dim constellations,
moonlight, and the Milky Way—

all eclipsed. In absolute dark
the ice dome, like a great cornea,

stares outward, unmoved.

White Earth and Ruins

> It all belies our existence; we wait, and are still denied.
> We are folded together, men and the snowy ground into nullity.
> There is silence, only the silence, never a sound or a verity
> to assist us, disastrously silence-bound.
>
> —D. H. LAWRENCE, from "Winter Lull"

Ernest Wild, February 27–29, 1916

It's 30 below. I roll a tea cigarette. Sing.
We'll return for you in four days, Joyce said.
It's our fourth day. No sign the storm will subside.
Food's gone. No fuel. God knows how the Padre
lives on. *Mors certa, hora incerta*, he reminds me.
Mack's sullen. Merciless winds howl outside.
In this half-light, days and nights bleed together.
I read. The Padre wakes from a dream and asks
after the weather. Shrieking, the blizzard replies.
It all belies our existence; we wait, and are still denied.

Day five. All is nothing but this tent, and the white
continent, though Padre mutters, *faith*. To keep him
lucid, I argue God, and he answers with such sincerity
of heart I cannot bait him anymore. His body's melted
a foot down into the bloodied puddle beneath him. He prays.
I sing. Before his frost-bitten hands lose all dexterity,
Mack scrawls a page, reports the job done, says farewell
to all he loves, then drops back into his sodden bag. Scott
and his team died near here. Facing that possibility,
we are folded together, men and the snowy ground into nullity.

The sixth day. Katabatic winds. Banshees all about.
Scurvy's blackening my legs. The Padre lies still
but for spasms which now, thank God, are a rarity.
When he speaks, if at all, it is to ask after Mack.
Mack drifts in and out, dazed, until something odd

rouses him. I am slow to recognize the new peculiarity,
but he shifts up onto his elbow, listening. The tent's
gone limp. An uncanny quiet. The stillness is so dense
I think snow's sealed us up so I crawl outside warily.
There is silence, only the silence, never a sound or a verity

except I see the black rag tied high on the pole
has fallen slack. All around the world's expanded,
stretched to an emptiness made more profound
in this deathly calm. I dig out the tent until the lull
is over. When the winds come on again, I go in
to sleep, spent. And then—how long?—a faint sound
pierces my crazed dreams and the droning wind—
Dogs yelping! I gather up a harness, crawl out, totter
toward Joyce and the others who've come 'round
to assist us, disastrously silence bound.

Richards

When I think of Wild, that sterling fellow,
how he came out, after all those days where we'd left him

without a crumb to look after the Padre and Mack—
to see him pick up his harness

and come a distance to meet us, to give *us* a hand—
    I cannot name my feelings.

The Breath of Night

From caves of ice and fields of snow
The breath of night like death did flow.
—PERCY BYSSHE SHELLEY, "The Cold Earth Slept Below"

The sun spirals low.
Blue swaths and shadows
paint the boundless ice.

Cool-headed Richards fell
to pieces when Wild emerged
from the tent, walked toward him,
then without a word, slipped
a harness over his head and helped
drag the sledge the last yards.
The men lifted Spencer-Smith's
frail body onto the sledge, fastened
him in. Mack, scuttled forward,
hunched, determined to remain
on his feet, but scurvy locked
his legs at right angles.

Here, everything is ice and snow
storm scrubbed, purified.
Everything here echoes *no*.

Hut Point is seventy-five
frigid miles away. Wild, Joyce,
and Richards haul the other three
men: Hayward, hypothermic,
incoherent; Spencer-Smith, helpless,
seldom conscious; and Mack,
who tumbles from the sledge
several times, and begs to be left
where he falls.

Slowly, the sun and a crescent
moon circle one another,
like old adversaries or lovers.

Eight days they pull their men,
lash bamboo poles to the backs
of their own legs against scurvy

drawing tendons back as they rest.
Sopping reindeer bags. Molting
fur sticks in their throats.

Ice gives nothing. It removes,
erases, fractures, reflects.
Ice creates one thing: more ice.

Joyce and Richards see
their one hope to save the Padre
is to leave behind the weight
of one man so they have the strength
to slog Spencer-Smith to safety.
Mack volunteers. They set him up
in one of the two tents and pull away.

It is the eighth of March.
Nearly the twilight season.
The sun sinks lower each day.

Five Men in a Three-Man Tent, Twenty-Eight Below Zero

Twenty Miles from Hut Point, March 9, 1916

Spencer-Smith finds the opium,
swallows a tablet.
This time he dreams
he's punting at Cambridge,
following a curve in the river.
His pole finds bottom, and he
presses forward. Autumn leaves
float and turn on the sun-spangled
water. So much sparkles, quickening.
Trees bluster, a fluster of ducks
flurry skyward, a swan hammers
against the punt. *I say, Rich,*
he calls out, *if your heart's behaving
funny, what's the best thing to do,
sit up or lie down?*
Richards replies that he doesn't know
but thinks it best to lie still.
Spencer-Smith imagines himself
fastening his black cassock,
fingering its thirty-nine buttons
for the Articles of Religion.

Two hours later ice crystals glitter
on his eyelashes and beard.
The men claw a shallow depression
in the ice. Too weak to lift the Padre,
they roll his body in, cover him
with a snow cairn. The cross made
of bamboo poles becomes a slight
smudge, then vanishes against
the white void behind them.

Gladys Mackintosh, the Second Spring

Bedford, March 1916

The blackthorns are blooming their clouds of white.
The sun's thin, but it's spring again, darling.

Little Pamela hugs daffodils, clutching them tight,

and the blackthorns are blooming. Clouds of white
drift in a bluebell sky. I wish I could write

to tell you the warblers are warbling
and the blackthorns are blooming their clouds of white.

The sun's thin but it's spring again, darling.

Left Behind, Mack's Sixth Day on the Ice

> What is that noise?
> The wind under the door.
> What is that noise now? What is the wind doing?
> Nothing again nothing.
>
> —T. S. ELIOT, "The Waste Land"

Delirious, alone, Mack bleeds
from his bowels, his legs are black,
bent by scurvy which destroys
tissue, loosens teeth. Mack rouses
to a shrieking wind. He calls out,
believing he hears his wife's voice—
Gladys, dear, is that you? His eye
shifts. His ears strain, listening
for the return of Joyce.
What is that noise?

My God! Shackleton?
I am more than pleased you're here!
Mack's hands slap the floor,
searching. *Where are my sticks?*
The winds pause, the tent walls
relax. Utter stillness. Then, a roar
and the canvas balloons taut, snaps
inward like cheeks sucked hollow,
inflates again, and tears open for
the wind under the door.

Snow shoves in and Mack
struggles to make a rough repair.
He feels his blistered hands going
numb. His mind unspools, haunted
by India. The indigo plantation.
Elephants like ships. Mother moving
the children back to England. He wrote

often to his father, who saved every letter,
unopened. Memory is confusing.
What is that noise now? What is the wind doing?

He calls out, *Who's there?*
The tent is a speck in a vast, white
void; frail shelter pitched in stunning
isolation. The phantom voices quiet.
Mack crawls from his reindeer bag
and hobbles outside clutching
his sticks. He squints, scans the far
distance for a smudge on the ice,
any sign that his men are coming.
Nothing again nothing.

Splice the Mainbrace

Joseph Stenhouse, March 14, 1916

Three hundred twenty-one days
and now, at last, we're free.

Heaven should hang a halo
on the head of Mr. Stephen
who built this ship strong enough
to sail through a frozen hell.

Let's have three blasts of the whistle boys—
three blasts of farewell to the ice.

In the Dark Time

> In the dark time of the year.
> Between melting and freezing
> —T. S. ELIOT, "Little Gidding"

Richard Richards, March 1916

After burying Smithy, Hayward closed down entirely.
It was all we could do to carry on, drag him to Hut Point.
When we got close, I heard a seal colony grunting

and from the deepest pit inside myself a manic urge
came over me. I wanted nothing more than to rush a seal
and pierce its throat. My body screamed for blood,

but we pressed on the last miles to get Hayward in.
The hut door was solidly iced up, so we hacked open
the window and managed to pass Hayward inside.

Wild and I found two seals; stunned them, sliced them up
and gave the pieces to Joyce to cook for us and the dogs.
The dogs had saved us again. Old Oscar is king of them all.

❋

Seal meat, in small doses, slowly restored us. We slaughtered
more seals, mended tent rips, overhauled the sledge, patched
our clothes with food-bags. We left Hayward in the hut,

headed out, the vision of Mack alone on the barrier whipping
us back to the south. I've never known a bond such I felt
for Wild and Joyce as we trudged past Smithy's grave.

On the third day, Joycey lifted the glasses and shouted,
I see him! He's all right! There outside the tent was Mack,
leaning on his pole gazing northward, listening for the dogs.

Nine long days alone had marked Mack. He'd written
his farewell letters. We found him peculiar, too dazed
to take in Smithy's death, or that the *Aurora* was likely lost.

❀

We made him eat a bit, hauled him north and three days
later, after the sun had gone down, laid him by Hayward,
who was little changed. Huddled around the blubber fire

I ran the computations through my mind. We'd done it.
Two hundred days. Hauled 4,500 pounds of supplies
more than 1,330 miles during this second season.

Shackleton had told Mack if his party wasn't in sight of the hut
by March 20, this very day, they were likely dead. In the evening,
I examined my limbs. Once Mack saw our own bitten faces,

weedy limbs, and swollen gums, that scurvy had blackened
our legs too, he stirred from his fog, solemnly gripped each man's
hand in turn, thanked us for laying the depots. For saving his life.

TO ICE

April 1916–January 1917

APRIL 15, 1916. Shackleton's three lifeboats land his party on Elephant Island, the first solid ground his men have stood on in 497 days.

MAY 20, 1916. Shackleton reaches Stromness whaling station. All his party are alive and rescued by August 30, 1916.

And what you thought you came for
Is only a shell, a husk of meaning
From which the purpose breaks only when it is fulfilled
If at all. Either you had no purpose
Or the purpose is beyond the end you figured
And is altered in fulfillment. There are other places
Which also are the world's end, some at the sea jaws,
Or over a dark lake, in a desert or a city—
But this is the nearest, in place and time,
Now and in England.
>   —T. S. ELIOT, "Little Gidding"

> No more remarkable story of human endeavor has been revealed than the tale of that long march.
>   —ERNEST SHACKLETON, speaking of the Ross Sea party

Seal Meat, Morning, Noon & Night

Ross Sea Party, Antarctica, April 1916

Joyce says he's as happy at Discovery Hut
as a "Piccadilly masher" now the job
is done. Nights, and day after day, it's dark
as a jackdaw. Wild and Richards hunt seal.
Slowly, the invalids recover, swollen black
gums recede. As blubber burns, smoke clouds

the iced-filled shack. Wind blasts clouds
of snow through gaps in the walls of the hut.
The men huddle in their bags, bodies black
from soot, greasy clothes deteriorating, the job
of washing impossible. Filthy, they lie sealed
in, toss blubber bricks on the stove in the dark

for heat, and doze. They're entirely in the dark
about their ship, about Shackleton, and the clouds
of German gas drifting over Ypres. A tin with seal
oil, rigged with a string, is the one lamp in the hut.
Mack sometimes struggles up and makes a fair job
of hobbling outside. He tries to shake his black

mood, but abhors their feral state. The sea's black.
Again, a gale has blown the ice away. With his dark,
scurvy-crippled legs and the relentless cold, it's a job
to remember his life before—gardens, lofty clouds
in a summer sky, the smell of soap. Discovery Hut
is just bearable for Hayward now he has seal

meat to restore himself. Joyce serves up seal
breakfast, lunch, and dinner. Meals of blackened
meat hunks are the high events in the hut.
Cape Evans, thirteen miles off, where the dark

weeks could pass as easily as scudding clouds,
taunts Mack. Watching sea-ice becomes his job.

Ill-tempered, Mack wills the ice to thicken so the job
of sledging across can begin. Joyce tallies the seal
supply, notes wind direction. Worries don't cloud
his mind; they're safe and eating. The black
flesh on the skipper's legs is improving. The dark
and squalor and stench inside Discovery Hut,

the thick clouds of smoke, are all part of the job
in a primitive polar hut when seal meat is all
there is in the black months of winter's dark.

The Men Asleep at the Bottom of the World

[*cento from poetry by Siegfried Sassoon, Wilfred Owen, Rupert Brook, and D. H. Lawrence*]

Hut Point, Antarctica May 1916

Fumbling, drunk with fatigue
the men totter towards rest.
   Lay shuddering. Sleep.

Darkness. Wraiths of green—aqueous, floating
   queer green light streaming
as under a green sea
     and someone dreamed green
leaves. Grass.
   The sweet hush after the talk of birds.

Someone moaned
dreaming of the benison of hot water.
   Clean beds. The cool kindliness of sheets.

Someone stirred, shifting his body, heard
softly, a woman singing. Remembered
   —a child under the piano,
   a mother who smiles as she sings.

Things with balls and bats.
    Old Sunday evenings at home.
Children at the table. Simple, homely crust
   of friendly bread and many-tasting food.
White plates and cups, clean-gleaming, ringed with blue.

   Hair's fragrance. The scent of limes
in bloom. In the flowing dress. Tenderness.
The throb and ache, the thumping heart.
    Come back. Come back.

And the astonishment of bustling life—
bank-holidays, picture shows, and spats.
Going to the office in the train.
      The deep-panting train.

Falling seeds of rain. Water dimpling.
    Deeps of melting blue and green water.
Dreams flicker. Fade. Dwindle as the wave goes home.

And this heart, where glory burns, slept. And this heart, lost
    among the stars, slept.
This heart drifting,
    dipped contented oars, sighed. And slept.

Waste

Ernest Wild, May 8, 1916

For forty days, we hauled the Padre,
that refined man with his easy habit
for delight, and watched him slowly melt
to whatever clarity a good soul can reach.

He bore it all quietly. Often, he apologized.
Some days, he slid from consciousness.
Some, he dissolved to a slender sob
when we lifted him, helpless onto the sledge.

In the end, we had to bury him in the ice,
far from the swans and swallows
of Cambridge, the green rivers
and soft rains, far from the sanctuary
of his church and family.

And now, Mack and Hayward,
two men we worked our guts out
to save, decide to play chances—
in spite of our protests, in spite of young ice
and a blizzard threatening—
announce they're off to Cape Evans today.

Mack says they'll travel light, not take
bags or tent or food, believes they'll make
the thirteen miles in less than eight hours.

Joyce forced a bag of seal meat and some
chocolate on them. Mack tucked his diary
in a pocket. Hayward cut Ethel's photo
from his diary and stuffed it in his blouse.

Now, Richards and Joyce and I watch
from the hill overlooking the sound.
The two figures shrink to dots on the vast
waste of ice. And then, they are gone.

Leaving Discovery Hut for Cape Evans

Richard Richards, July 1916

Our minds furred, half-frozen,
we were burrowed animals

waiting months,
crouched, staring into

the sputtering blubber fire.
We waited, muttering

over whether or not
Shackleton had perished,

whether or not
our ship had returned,

wanting to know if
Mack and Hayward survived.

We waited, gnawing
on greasy seal meat,

for the ice to grow thick,
for the moon to grow full.

And when the ice
thickened and the moon

was fat and bright
we emerged, blinking,

stinking of smoke,
of blubber and blood,

and together, we three
black cinders and the last

four dogs made our way
across the ice

now iron hard,
into the silvered night.

❊

We trekked across the ice
following the same route

Mack and Hayward used
in May. Joyce, Wild, and I

had gone nearly six
of the thirteen miles

when the full moon's light
guttered like a candle.

Joyce cried out
By God—look!

And we saw our moon
eclipsed, pared down

to a slim lune. We traveled on
in deep shadow for hours

until through the gloom
came the sound of dogs

and Towser, Con,
Oscar, and Gunner

bounded forward,
yelping in reply

and men, silhouetted
by the returning

moonlight, waved
from the hut

we hadn't seen
in ten long months,

and pups born
in that time to the bitch

we'd all forgotten,
whined and leapt

as we were welcomed
into the blinding yellow light.

Gladys Mackintosh in the Garden

Bedford, England, August 1916

These days if the chemist's boy peddles down the lane
curtains brush back and we all wonder who
will read *I regret to inform you. It gives me great pain* . . .

So today when the chemist's boy turns down our lane
I rise from the roses, shield my brow and strain
to see his face. Perhaps he's delivering a tonic. It isn't true.

I can see it's a telegram the boy's peddling down the lane.
Every curtain's brushed back. In a moment we'll know who.

Marking Time

Ernest Wild, Cape Evans, July 1916—January 1917

When the other dogs attacked Con,
there was no saving him.
Joyce couldn't stop the bleeding
so we buried that fine dog in July.
It was an awful blow to Joycey
though nothing bothered him ever
so much as when Richards
went down in August. Richy cried out,
his arms flew up, and he dropped
like an anchor to the floor.
It absolutely shattered Joycey.

Cope says Richy's heart is strained.
We set him up in Captain Scott's
old bunk. He's still weak on his pins,
but Cope's bunked in close by,
caring after him and healing
himself in the bargain. Since May,
Cope had been right off his head.
Refused food. Curled in a corner.
Muttered on about murderers
so we hid away the harpoon gun.

❀

Joyce was anxious to leave the hut
so one October day we took ourselves
to Cape Royds, seven miles away.
Turned up a bounty there, left behind
by Captain Scott. Cases of salmon.
Haddock and butter. Eight years old
and still splendid. A large case

94

of Bryant & May's matches,
but to my great sorrow, no tobacco.

The scientists keep busy. Proved
their worth by cooking up beer
from malt yeast and alcohol.
Made us all sociable and jolly
until the aftereffects.

Every four hours, 'round the clock
sour-face Stevens slogs up
Wind Vane Hill for his temperature
and wind readings. He was left back
six months whilst we were on the ice.
Mack called Stevens a layabout,
that he was always swinging the lead,
but Cope said he was feeling poorly.
And, all alone, thin as a straw, Stevens
kept up his observations. It's a wonder
the fearsome winds didn't whisk
that surly Scotsman off like a rag.

❊

Since the grand old sun returned,
we've searched many a time
along the coast for a trace of Mack
and Hayward. Gaze and Jack
are building a cross to set up
at the Padre's grave with his name
carved in the wood and the words
a brave man.

Joyce believes we're stuck here
for another year so we keep sealing
for meat and fuel. Once my ricked foot

mended I came to live at Cape Royds
to help Joyce with his zoological
collection. On one of the walls,
he's painted *Joyce's Skinning Academy.*
Killed and skinned to date: 10 Skua;
50 Emperors. 10 Adelies, 10 young.
3 Sea leopards. 2 giant petrals.
Also collected: 3,150 penguin eggs.

In two weeks, I'll go back to Cape Evans.
Joycey wants his solitude.
Often, he'll speculate on the *Aurora's* fate,
on what's become of Shackleton
and my brother Frank; if the war's still on.
Time better spent finding eggs.

Ship Ho!

Richards sees it first.
It materializes from the mist
as he holds the glasses to his eyes
scanning for seals. A drifting berg,
he thinks, until a curl of smoke
rises from it into the northern sky.

At the breakfast table he passes
a quiet word to Joyce, who goes
to the high window. Standing on a box,
Joyce peers across the frozen sound
to the spot nine miles off. Blinks.
Then he shouts

Ship Ho!   97

A clatter of crockery, scraped chairs,
cries and calls, backs clapped,
a confusion of what to grab first,
so they grab each other, quaking,
grip hands and shake hard.

The outline of the ship sharpens
as they dash toward it with dogs
and loaded sledges. It can't be.
It is! They whoop their joy
recognizing the *Aurora*.

Joyce beams with the binoculars
held tight to his eyes. A mile or so
across the ice three small figures
like penguins materialize,

come toward them and he knows,
is dead sure, one of the figures
walks exactly like Shackleton.

Joyce, old man. I am more than pleased to see you.

And there he is, The Boss, large as life,
standing here, hand extended.

In such a moment perhaps nothing seems
quite real, but the mind may just crack
open enough to allow a narrow glimpse
of something warm. Something clean.

The men are filthy. They've worn the same
clothes for more than two years. The stench
of their bodies is fierce. Wild-eyed, manic,
they burble, blurt a frenzy of words.

Hoot. Weep. Jack too overcome
to leave the hut, remains fluttering
inside, fussing, petting his things.

How many men have we lost?

Once The Boss is told about Mackintosh
and Hayward, about Spencer-Smith,
Shackleton sends the prearranged signal
to Captain John King Davis on the *Aurora*,
who instantly understands three men perished
when Shackleton and his two shipmates
move apart and all three lie down flat on the ice.

To Ice

after Brian Turner's "To Sand"

To ice, four thousand pounds of food.
    To ice the sledge dogs go.

To ice, the gangrene parts, the wits of men
    in the months-long dark,

in the blood-drenched snow. To ice, the frosted spar
    and beam, a slurry sea, a mountain range.

To ice, our ghosts: The Padre, Hayward, Mack.

To ice, an entire continent.
    Ice is cause and consequence—

all ice touches it becomes.
    At the vortex, time itself succumbs.

NOTES

AENEAS LIONEL ACTON MACKINTOSH ("Mack")—Age 35, Commander of the *Aurora*. Born in India, son of a Scottish indigo planter. Mackintosh was a naval officer and had accompanied Shackleton on the *Nimrod* expedition, the expedition which cost Mack his right eye in an accident.

JOSEPH RUSSELL STENHOUSE—Age 27, First Officer of the *Aurora* and ship's captain while Mackintosh sledged. A Scotsman from a prosperous shipbuilding family, he was hired on by Shackleton from the British India Steam Navigation Company.

ERNEST EDWARD JOYCE—Age 39, recruited by Shackleton to be in charge of "sledging equipment and dogs." Joyce was a Royal Naval seaman who began his career as a boy. A *Nimrod* expedition veteran and experienced sledger, this was his fourth voyage to Antarctica.

HARRY ERNEST WILD—Age 35, hired on as storekeeper for the *Aurora*. A British Royal Navy seaman, he was recommended to Shackleton by his brother, Frank Wild, who was second-in-command on the *Endurance*.

REVEREND ARNOLD SPENCER-SMITH ("The Padre")—Age 31, chaplain and photographer. A Scottish Episcopal priest and schoolmaster who was a last-minute replacement as expeditionary photographer.

VICTOR GEORGE HAYWARD—Age 27, general assistant. A recently engaged London accounts clerk hired on because he had some experience working with sledging dogs on a ranch in Canada.

RICHARD WALTER RICHARDS—Age 22, an Australian physics teacher looking for adventure and selected to be part of the scientific team on the *Aurora*.

THE SCIENTIFIC TEAM occasionally helped with sledging duties, and carried out biological, meteorological, and magnetic research working from the Cape Evans hut. In addition to Richards, the team included: John Cope, a 21-year-old biologist and ship's medical officer; Alexander Stevens, a Scottish geologist; and Keith Jack, an industrial chemist.

SY *AURORA* was built in 1876 in Scotland for the Dundee Seal and Whale Fishing Company and sailed in the North Atlantic until 1910. Between 1911 and 1917, she made five trips to Antarctica. Last seen carrying coal from New South Wales to Chile, the *Aurora* was posted as missing, believed to be a casualty of a World War I German mine.

DISCOVERY HUT is located at Hut Point, a long, narrow peninsula on Ross Island. It is a square wooden structure built to serve as a storehouse and emergency shelter for the *Discovery* expedition of 1901–1904. It was never intended to be living quarters, therefore, was marginally insulated and lacked sleeping bunks.

CAPE EVANS HUT is located on the north shore of Cape Evans on Ross Island. It is a 50 by 25 ft., well-insulated structure lit with acetylene gas. Coal stoves furnished heat. The hut included a kitchen, utility and storage areas, sleeping bunks, general work area, and a dark room.

MINNA BLUFF is a key landmark for Antarctic expeditions. It is a rocky promontory at the eastern end of a peninsula projecting into the Ross Ice Shelf.

MOUNT HOPE is a dome-shaped hill, 3,500 feet high, situated at the base of the Beardmore Glacier. Named by Shackleton in 1908 during the *Nimrod* expedition, his ascent of Mount Hope offered the first view of the glacier that would provide a route to the South Pole.

SOURCE NOTES

"One Audacious Idea" epigraph from the *London Times*.

"Trapped Returning, the Twelve Day Blizzard" epigraph and italicized passages in "Five Men in a Three-Man Tent, Twenty-Eight Below Zero" from Kelly Tyler-Lewis, *The Lost Men: The Harrowing Saga of Shackleton's Ross Sea Party* (New York: Penguin Books, 2006).

"The Race to Minna Bluff" italicized passages from "The Spell of the Yukon" by Robert W. Service.

"A Glimpse of Hell" and "The Red Comet" epigraphs from Stephen Haddelsey, *Ice Captain: The Life of J. R. Stenhouse* (Gloucestershire, UK: History, 2008).

"Spencer-Smith's Woodbines" erasure from "Cigarettes" by B. H. Fairchild.

"Wild's Hut Point Mixture" epigraph and all italicized passages from original diary entries from Wilson McOrist, *Shackleton's Heroes: The Epic Story of the Men Who Kept the Endurance Expedition Alive* (New York: Skyhorse Publishing, 2016).

"The Golden Gateway, Final Depot 83° 31′ S" epigraph and italicized passages and specimen list from Ernest E. Mills Joyce, *The South Polar Trail* (London: Duckworth, 1929; reprint by Delhi, India: Facsimile, 2015).

"The Cold, Quiescent Eye" title phrase from Stephen J. Pyne, *The Ice: A Journey to Antarctica* (University of Iowa City Press, Iowa City, 1988).

"The Men Asleep at the Bottom of the World," cento passages from Siegfried Sassoon, "The Last Meeting," "Dreamers," "Glory of Women," "The Death Bed," "The Soldier"; Wilfred Owen, "Anthem for Doomed Youth," "Dulce et Decorum Est"; Rupert Brook, "Retrospect," "The Great Lover"; D. H. Lawrence, "The Piano," "Discord in Childhood."

ACKNOWLEDGMENTS

M any thanks to the editors of the following publications in which these poems appeared:

Common Threads: "Learning Detachment," "Penguins and Whales."

Dalhousie Review: "The Men Asleep at the Bottom of the World."

Escape into Life: "Frostbite, Last Team on the Barrier," "Gladys Mackintosh," "Gladys Mackintosh, the Second Spring," "The Lay of the Land," "Butchering Seals in the Dark," "The Sledging Commences," "Dead Dog Trail," "White Earth and Ruins."

Grey Sparrow Journal: "The Cold, Quiescent Eye."

Literary Nest: "Waiting for Deliverance," "Cape Evans Hut," "Gladys Mackintosh, Advent," "Seal Meat, Morning, Noon & Night," "Gladys Mackintosh in the Garden."

Main Street Rag: "Iceberg, Departing."

Mezzo Cammin: "Relaying the Load," "Spencer-Smith's Woodbines."

Parhelion Literary Magazine: "Beyond the Narwhal Gate," "Five Men in a Three-Man Tent, Twenty-Eight Below Zero," "Left Behind, Mack's Sixth Day on the Ice," "Ship Ho!."

Pedestal Magazine and selected for Antarctic 2020 Poetry Exhibition, Antarctica: "All My Flowers."

Rabbit: "Southing."

Sheila-Na-Gig: "Two Hundred Fifty Miles Out, Nine Day Coal Supply," "Rudder-less."

Tishman Review: "Perhaps I Was Eden"

I am deeply grateful to Carol V. Davis for selecting my book as winner of the 2021 Wheelbarrow Books Poetry Prize, and to Anita Skeen, series editor for Michigan State University's Wheelbarrow Books, for their encouragement and enthusiastic support of *Ice Hours*.

Many thanks to Amanda Frost at Michigan State University Press for her diligence and care preparing this book.

Appreciation and praise for Erin Kirk's artistry in creating the cover design.

Heartfelt gratitude to Barbara Sabol for reading the book and these poems many, many times, offering her keen wisdom and rousing encouragement, and for her steadfast love for the Ross Sea men and Antarctica's voice.

Thanks and love to the Sunday Group: Kit Almy, Gail Griffin, Christine Horton, Gail Martin, and Susan Ramsey, for their brilliant critiques, for their encouragement, and sticking with me long distance.

Blessings on the Kalamazoo Dawgs for their insights and generosity as they responded to poems in this collection.

Sincere appreciation to Conor Bracken who read the book deeply and thoughtfully and helped me burnish it by offering his astute guidance and enthusiasm for the project.

SERIES ACKNOWLEDGMENTS

We at Wheelbarrow Books have many people to thank without whom *Ice Hours* would never be in your hands. We begin by thanking all those writers who submitted manuscripts to the eleventh Wheelbarrow Books Prize for Poetry. We want to single out the finalists, Donald Levering, Jed Myers, Christine Rhein, and Tina Schumann, whose manuscripts moved and delighted us and which we passed onto the competition judge, Carol V. Davis, for her final selection.

Our thanks to Kelsey Block, Laura Horan, Natalie Mannino, and Estee Schlenner for their careful reading of manuscripts and insightful commentary on their selections, and especially to Laurie Hollinger, assistant director at the RCAH Center for Poetry, who also read the manuscripts and provided the logistical aid and financial wizardry for this project.

Then we go on to thank Stephen Esquith, dean of the Residential College in the Arts and Humanities, who gave his initial support to the Center for Poetry and Wheelbarrow Books, and current interim dean, Dylan Miner. Conversation with June Youatt, former provost at Michigan State University, was encouraging and MSU Press director Gabriel Dotto and assistant director Julie Loehr were eager to support the efforts of poets to continue reaching an eager audience. Thanks also to Lauren Russell, director of the RCAH Center for Poetry, for her support of Wheelbarrow Books. We cannot thank you enough for having the faith in us, and the love of literature, to collaborate on this project.

Thanks to our current Editorial Board, Sarah Bagby, Gabrielle Calvocoressi, Leila Chatti, Carol V. Davis, Mark Doty, George Ellenbogen, Carolyn Forche, George Ella Lyon, Thomas Lynch, and Naomi Shihab Nye for believing Wheelbarrow Books was a worthy undertaking and lending their support and their time to our success.

Finally, to our patrons: Without your belief in the Wheelbarrow Books Series and your generous financial backing, we would still be sitting around the conference table adding up our loose change. You are making it possible for poets, when publishing a new volume of poetry is becoming harder and harder these days with so many presses discontinuing their publishing of poetry, to find an outlet for their work as well as supporting the efforts of established poets to continue to reach a large and grateful audience. We name you here with great admiration and appreciation:

Beth Alexander   Fred Kraft

Gayle Davis   Jean Kreuger

Mary Hayden   Brain Teppen

Patricia and Robert Miller

There are many others whose smaller contributions we value whether those contributions come in terms of dollars, support for our programming, or promoting the books we have published and the writers we treasure. Thank you, one and all.

WHEELBARROW BOOKS

Anita Skeen, *Series Editor*

Sarah Bagby

Gabrielle Calvocoressi

Leila Chatti

Carol V. Davis

Mark Doty

George Ellenbogen

Carolyn Forché

Thomas Lynch

Naomi Shihab Nye

George Ella Lyon

Wheelbarrow Books, established in 2016, is an imprint of the RCAH Center for Poetry at Michigan State University, published and distributed by MSU Press. The biannual Wheelbarrow Books Poetry Prize is awarded every year to one emerging poet who has not yet published a first book and to one established poet.

SERIES EDITOR: Anita Skeen, professor in the Residential College in the Arts and Humanities (RCAH) at Michigan State University, founder and past director of the RCAH Center for Poetry, director of the Creative Arts Festival at Ghost Ranch, and director of the Fall Writing Festival

The RCAH Center for Poetry opened in the fall of 2007 to encourage the reading, writing, and discussion of poetry and to create an awareness of the place and power of poetry in our everyday lives. We conceive of this broadly— including through readings, performances, workshops, contests, interdisciplinary conversations, and engagement with communities. We believe that poetry is and should be fun, accessible, and meaningful. Through its many manifestations, poetry also has the potential to raise awareness, stimulate new ways of thinking and knowing, and galvanize change. We are building a poetry community in the Greater Lansing area and beyond. Our undertaking of the Wheelbarrow Books Poetry Series is one of the gestures we make to aid in connecting good writers and eager readers beyond our regional boundaries. Information about the RCAH

Center for Poetry at MSU can be found at http://poetry.rcah.msu.edu and also on Instagram, Facebook, and Twitter (@CenterForPoetry).

The mission of the Residential College in the Arts and Humanities at Michigan State University is to weave together the passion, imagination, humor, and candor of the arts and humanities to promote individual well-being and the common good. Students, faculty, and community partners in the arts and humanities have the power to focus critical attention on the public issues we face and the opportunities we have to resolve them. The arts and humanities not only give us the pleasure of living in the moment but also the wisdom to make sound judgments and good choices.

The mission, then, is to see things as they are, to hear things as others may, to tell these stories as they should be told, and to contribute to the making of a better world. The Residential College in the Arts and Humanities is built on four cornerstones: world history, art and culture, ethics, and engaged learning. Together they define an open-minded public space within which students, faculty, staff, and community partners can explore today's common problems and create shared moral visions of the future. Discover more about the Residential College in the Arts and Humanities at Michigan State at http://rcah.msu.edu.